NARRATIVE
NONFICTION

CALVIN GRAHAM'S WORLD WAR II STORY

KATIE MARSICO
ILLUSTRATED BY DAVE HILL

Lerner Publications ◆ Minneapolis

PUBLISHER'S NOTE

This story is based on historical events. The people, places, and dates are known through primary source accounts of the time. While inspired by known facts, dialogue and some descriptive details have been fictionalized.

To the O'Hallorans—thanks for everything you do for our country!

Copyright © 2018 by Lerner Publishing Group, Inc.

All rights reserved. International copyright secured. No part of this book may be reproduced, stored in a retrieval system, or transmitted in any form or by any means—electronic, mechanical, photocopying, recording, or otherwise—without the prior written permission of Lerner Publishing Group, Inc., except for the inclusion of brief quotations in an acknowledged review.

Lerner Publications Company
A division of Lerner Publishing Group, Inc.
241 First Avenue North
Minneapolis, MN 55401 USA

For reading levels and more information, look up this title at www.lernerbooks.com.

The images in this book are used with the permission of: US Navy photographer/Wikimedia Commons (Public Domain), p. 30 (Calvin Graham); NH 80-G-36088 courtesy of the Naval History & Heritage Command, p. 30 (ship); OneSmallSquare/Shutterstock.com, p. 31.

Main body text set in Rotis Serif Std 55 Regular 15/24.
Typeface provided by Adobe Systems.

Library of Congress Cataloging-in-Publication Data

Names: Marsico, Katie, 1980– author.
Title: Calvin Graham's World War II story / Katie Marsico.
Description: Minneapolis : Lerner Publications, [2018] | Series: Narrative nonfiction : Kids in war | Includes bibliographical references. | Audience: K to Grade 3. | Audience: Ages 7-9.
Identifiers: LCCN 2017004834 (print) | LCCN 2017013818 (ebook) | ISBN 9781512497816 (eb pdf) | ISBN 9781512456813 (library binding : alk. paper)
Subjects: LCSH: Graham, Calvin, 1930–1992 | World War, 1939-1945—Campaigns—Pacific Area—Juvenile literature. | Sailors—United States—Juvenile literature. | South Dakota (Battleship : BB-57)—Juvenile literature. | United States. Navy—Juvenile literature. | Child soldiers—United States—Biography—Juvenile literature. | World War, 1939-1945—Participation, Juvenile—Juvenile literature.
Classification: LCC D767 (ebook) | LCC D767 .M258 2018 (print) | DDC 940.54/265933092 [B]—dc23

LC record available at https://lccn.loc.gov/2017004834

Manufactured in the United States of America
1-42950-26766-8/2/2017

FOREWORD

From 1939 to 1945, the Allies and the Axis powers battled each other during World War II. The United States was an Allied nation, while the main Axis nations were Germany, Japan, and Italy. By August 1942, the US Navy was desperate for new seamen. Calvin Graham left his home in Crockett, Texas, at the age of eleven. He was so eager to fight in the war that he pretended he was seventeen and joined the navy. He was soon called to San Diego, California, for training.

As World War II went on, several important naval battles occurred in the South Pacific Ocean. One was the Naval Battle of Guadalcanal in November 1942. US and Japanese forces were fighting for control of an airfield on Guadalcanal Island.

NOVEMBER 14, 1942, THE SOUTH PACIFIC

During the final hours of November 14, 1942, Calvin Graham watched smoke billow above the South Pacific. At times, he heard the whir of gunfire or the thunder of a torpedo blast. Then the thick, gray clouds glowed orange, and screams echoed across the waves.

Calvin was manning a gun aboard the battleship USS *South Dakota*. As the Battle of Guadalcanal raged around him, he took aim at Japanese warships. It wasn't Calvin's first experience with naval warfare. In October, he had helped shoot planes out of the sky during the Battle of Santa Cruz. Yet it was the struggle for Guadalcanal that forever changed Calvin's life.

That night the *South Dakota* cruised near Guadalcanal's western tip in search of enemy ships. Then, at 11:33 p.m., the ship unexpectedly lost electrical power. Without radar, the crew found it difficult to track enemy movements. Calvin and his shipmates had little warning when the Japanese fired at them.

JAPAN

PACIFIC
OCEAN

HAWAIIAN
ISLANDS

GUADALCANAL

AUSTRALIA

NEW
ZEALAND

"Down!" a voice barked in Calvin's direction. For a few seconds, the whirlwind of noise and activity around him faded into silence. Suddenly, Japanese gunfire pounded into the *South Dakota*. Before Calvin could react, a flash of white-hot pain tore into his head. The force of another explosion tossed him backward like a rag doll. Calvin crashed through the deck and landed on his back, three stories below.

ALL HANDS ON DECK

The heat of the explosion had burned Calvin's face. Metal splinters, or shrapnel, had ripped into his flesh and knocked out his front teeth. Calvin didn't want to move. But he knew he couldn't just lay there. He tried to sit up. His head was pounding, and blood trickled from his mouth.

Calvin wasn't sure what had just happened. His senses were a blur. Minutes passed, and a sound grew clearer to him—the cries of his shipmates. For a moment, he wondered if he was having a nightmare.

"Graham, are you all right?" It was one of the medics aboard the *South Dakota*. He helped Calvin rise to his feet. "Good," he said briskly, once he was sure Calvin wasn't dying. "We'll need to treat you later of course. Perhaps a few stitches and something for the burns. But you *will* be all right, Graham. In the meantime, get back on deck. Everyone who can walk is needed. No shortage of wounded, I'm afraid!" As the medic spoke, another blast thudded against the ship. Calvin grabbed a railing to avoid falling over.

"All hands on deck, Seaman!" repeated the medic a bit more sternly. Without waiting to see if Calvin had obeyed him, he raced back up toward the main deck. Calvin trailed behind. He was determined to block out his pain and do his duty.

DEATH AND DESTRUCTION

Once Calvin climbed back on deck, he took a deep breath. No matter where he turned, he saw his shipmates. Some were moaning and calling for help. Others lay motionless and silent. As Calvin crouched alongside the first still body, a chill crept over him.

"No," Calvin muttered. "Not Red." Calvin checked for a pulse, but there was none. The seaman's face was barely recognizable. But Calvin knew who it was even before lifting the seaman's dog tags. They were charred, but Calvin could make out the name "Hezil." For a moment, Calvin thought he'd be sick to his stomach. Red Hezil had been his closest friend on the ship. They'd spent hours playing cards and talking about what they would do once the war ended.

Now Red was gone, and those times were over. Calvin's mind began to wander to the last conversation they had, but he was interrupted by something tugging at his shirt. He spun around to find one of his shipmates grabbing hold of him.

"Please," the man groaned. "My leg—it's bleeding. It won't stop, and the medics won't come. Please do something!" Even in the darkness, Calvin could see blood rushing from the man's leg. If the gush didn't slow, Calvin knew the man would die.

CARING FOR THE CREW

Calvin searched the deck around him. He desperately wished he had a tourniquet, or tight bandage, to stop the bleeding. During the Battle of Santa Cruz, Calvin had seen medics use tourniquets to save lives. Suddenly, he had an idea. He turned back to Red and started to remove his friend's belt.

"You'll be all right," Calvin said
to the man with the bleeding leg.
Calvin realized he was repeating the
same words the medic had spoken
to him. He twisted Red's belt into a
makeshift tourniquet and wound it
around the man's leg. All the while,
his jaw throbbed, and he struggled to
concentrate. The flow of blood slowed,
but in the darkness, Calvin couldn't
tell if it had stopped completely. As he
squinted at the wound, he felt a hand
on his shoulder.

"I'll take it from here, Graham," the medic told Calvin. He examined the man's leg and nodded approvingly. "Good work. Go see if you can find more belts. We're going to need extra tourniquets before the night is over."

"Yes, sir," Calvin said. He heard his shipmate groan, but the noise was soon drowned out by the sounds of fighting. As Calvin moved around the ship, he was aware of flickers and flashes out on the dark water. He knew that they were coming from burning warships. Calvin couldn't always tell if they were Japanese or American ships. Eventually, he ignored them as he went about his work.

While Calvin gathered belts, he comforted his injured shipmates by making conversation with them. It wasn't easy since his mouth was sore and swollen. Yet Calvin pushed past his pain to help distract the men from theirs.

OLD ENOUGH TO BE A HERO

As the night wore on, the sounds of combat grew fainter. Calvin guessed that the badly damaged *South Dakota* was heading away from the action. He wondered who was winning the battle. And he tried not to think about all the destruction he had just seen.

"Graham, over here," called the
medic. "It's your turn." The medic
studied Calvin's injuries, put ointment
on his burns, and gave him a few
stitches. Calvin did his best to stay
still, though his mind was racing.

"Sir," Calvin began. "It seems like we were hit pretty hard."

"The *South Dakota* will need to dock in New York for repair," the medic confirmed. "And yes, we suffered some losses. I don't know the exact numbers yet, but there are more than thirty dead." Calvin nodded, thinking of Red.

"But it's not all bad news," the medic continued. "The Japanese ships are in worse shape than we are. I'd say the odds of the enemy recapturing Guadalcanal just got lower." He trimmed Calvin's final stitch and then put down his scissors. The medic looked at Calvin as if he was trying to find the answer to a question. "I'm guessing the odds are also slim that your life will ever be the same after tonight."

Calvin lowered his eyes. Officially, he was still too young to serve. But he felt older than twelve. And he knew, even if the truth stayed secret, he was old enough to be a veteran—as well as a hero.

AFTERWORD

In November 1942, US forces won the Battle of Guadalcanal. The *South Dakota* arrived in New York the following month. At first, Calvin was treated as a war hero. He received a Bronze Star and a Purple Heart for his service in the South Pacific.

Not long afterward, however, Calvin's mother saw him in the news. She reported his true age to the navy, and he was stripped of his awards. Decades later, when people learned more about Calvin's story, these honors were restored to him. Calvin was one of the youngest US servicemen to participate in World War II.

April 3, 1930 Calvin Graham is born in
Canton, Texas.

1939–1945 Allied and Axis nations fight one
another in World War II.

August 15, 1942

Calvin joins the navy,
despite being underage.

October 1942 The *South Dakota* sees action
during the Battle of Santa Cruz.

November 14, 1942

Calvin is injured
during the Battle
of Guadalcanal but
still helps care for
wounded shipmates.

December 1942 The *South Dakota* arrives in
New York to be repaired. In the months that
follow, Calvin is honored as a military hero.

April 1943 After Calvin's mother informs US
officials of his age, he is stripped of his
honors and discharged from the navy.

1948–1951 Graham serves in the US Marine Corps.

1978 President Jimmy Carter orders that Graham's
military honors, except for the Purple Heart,
be restored to him.

November 6, 1992 Graham dies and is buried in
Fort Worth, Texas.

1994
Graham's family receives
his Purple Heart.

LEARN MORE ABOUT CALVIN GRAHAM

BOOKS

Enzo, George. *World War II in the Pacific: War with Japan.* New York: Cavendish Square, 2014. Read this book for a more detailed account of how World War II played out in the Pacific.

Newman, Patricia. *Navy SEALs: Elite Operations.* Minneapolis: Lerner Publications, 2014. Check out this book for an overview of what modern naval heroes do.

Townsend, John. *World War II: Navy.* London: Hachette Children's Books, 2013. Read this book for a closer look at the naval fleets that shaped World War II.

WEBSITES

Ducksters: World War II—The War in the Pacific
http://www.ducksters.com/history/world_war_ii/ww2_in_pacific.php
Visit this site for more information about World War II in the Pacific.

History for Kids: World War II Ships
http://www.historyforkids.net/world-war-2-ships.html
Head here for more information on the remarkable battleships used during World War II.

National Geographic Kids: Ten Eye-Opening Facts about World War II
http://www.ngkids.co.uk/history/world-war-two
Review a series of fast facts about the far-reaching conflict between Allied and Axis nations.